ATVs

By Jeff Savage

Consultant:
Doug Morris
Director
All Terrain Vehicle Association

Capstone
press

Mankato, Minnesota

Capstone High-Interest Books are published by Capstone Press
151 Good Counsel Drive, P.O. Box 669, Mankato, Minnesota 56002
www.capstonepress.com

Library of Congress Cataloging-in-Publication Data
Savage, Jeff, 1961–
 ATVs / by Jeff Savage.
  p. cm.—(Wild rides!)
  Summary: Provides an overview of the history and development of
all-terrain vehicles, their main features, and ATV competitions.
  Includes bibliographical references and index.
  ISBN 0-7368-2428-6 (hardcover)
  1. All-terrain vehicles—Juvenile literature. [1. All terrain
vehicles.] I. Title. II. Series.
TL235.6.S28 2004
629.22'042—dc22
                                                                        2003014555

Editorial Credits
James Anderson, editor; Kia Adams, series designer; Patrick D. Dentinger,
    book designer; Jo Miller, photo researcher

Photo Credits
Corbis/George D. Lepp, 26; Lester Lefkowitz, 25; Nick Wheeler, 10; Richard
    Hamilton Smith, 7
Getty Images/Al Bello, cover, 17; Francois Dubourg, 4, 14, 20, 22; Jamie Squire,
    18; Rick Wilking, 8; Time Life Pictures/Alan Levenson, 12
Photo courtesy of Julie Farr, 28

Table of Contents

Learn about:

ATV manufacturers

ATV costs

ATV uses

CHAPTER

ATVs

More than 200 ATV racers gather at the starting line to begin a cross-country race. The race starts on a beach. A race official waves the green flag, and the racers speed away from the starting line.

The racers zoom down the first straightaway at 50 miles (80 kilometers) an hour. They shift into lower gears and hit the brakes as they prepare for a sharp turn.

The racers grip the handlebars as they bounce over rocks and jumps. They splash their ATVs through a creek. One ATV stalls. The rest of the pack zips past. The racers zoom through the woods and then down another straightaway. After about 30 minutes, one lap is finished. The racers have four laps to go to complete the race.

About ATVs

ATV stands for all-terrain vehicle. ATVs are also called quads or four-wheelers. They can go safely over dirt, sand, rocks, snow, and mud. ATVs are built for everyone from ranchers to firefighters. Some ATVs are made just for kids.

Many companies around the world make ATVs. Some popular companies are Arctic Cat, Honda, Kawasaki, Polaris, Suzuki, and Yamaha. ATV companies sell about 800,000 ATVs each year.

The cost of an ATV varies. ATVs with small engines may cost $1,400 or less. Midlevel ATVs for pleasure riding or work cost about $3,400. Racing teams may spend $10,000 or more for high-performance ATVs.

Top racers modify high-performance ATVs. They sometimes spend another $10,000 or more to add racing parts to improve their ATVs.

Farmers and ranchers use ATVs to carry supplies.

In 2003, ATVs were used to search for parts of the space shuttle *Columbia* after it crashed.

ATVs in Action

About 8 million people in the United States ride ATVs. Firefighters and search-and-rescue teams ride ATVs to reach remote areas. Farmers use ATVs to travel between fields. Ranchers herd cattle with ATVs.

ATVs are popular with people who enjoy outdoor sports. Hunters, anglers, and campers can travel farther along trails on ATVs than they can driving cars or trucks.

People of all ages enjoy riding ATVs for fun. They ride in open fields or on long rides on off-road trails.

Some ATV riders become pro racers. They race on indoor and outdoor tracks. Races are held in stadiums, arenas, or on outdoor courses. Pro riders are awarded prizes for winning races. They also earn money from sponsors. Some sponsors pay racers to use their product or wear their logo during a race.

Learn about:

- **Honda ATC90**

- **Safety issues**

- **Four-wheelers**

CHAPTER 2

Early ATVs

ATVs were invented in Canada in the 1950s. These ATVs had six wheels. They were used by farmers to pull small wagons.

In 1967, workers at Honda Motor Company in Japan began designing an all-terrain vehicle. Osamu Takeuchi was the lead engineer.

Takeuchi and his team tried different shapes and sizes. They designed machines with three wheels, four wheels, and six wheels. They decided on a three-wheeled model. Honda's first ATVs were built in 1970. People called them three-wheelers.

Three-Wheelers

The first three-wheeler was the Honda US90. The Honda US90 sold for $595. Soon, Honda renamed it the ATC90. ATC stands for all-terrain cycle.

Three-wheelers tipped over easily.

People rushed to buy these new machines. A smaller version was built for kids. It was called the ATC70. In 1979, Honda introduced a more powerful vehicle called the ATC110. Soon, other companies built and sold three-wheelers.

ATV Changes

Three-wheelers were not very stable. They tipped over easily. Hospitals reported hundreds of emergency room visits each year due to ATV accidents.

In 1986, the U.S. Consumer Product Safety Commission got involved. This government group worked with ATV companies to make ATVs safer.

Two years later, the companies agreed to stop building three-wheelers. They agreed that only four-wheeled ATVs would be made. They offered classes to teach people how to drive ATVs safely. ATV riding became even more popular.

Learn about:

- **Frames**

- **Tires**

- **Engine sizes**

CHAPTER **3**

Designing an ATV

Manufacturers build different models of ATVs for different purposes. Most ATVs are built for pleasure riding. Some ATVs are work vehicles. Others are designed for sport. All ATVs have the same basic parts.

Basic Parts

Most of an ATV's parts connect to a chassis, or frame. Most ATV frames are made of steel. Racing frames are made of chromoly. This metal is a mixture of two metals called chromium and molybdenum. Chromoly is sturdy and lightweight.

An ATV's handlebars are similar to the handlebars of a motorcycle. The throttle is always on the right handlebar.

ATVs have several gears for different speeds and terrain. The transmission allows the driver to shift gears. The ATV can have a manual or an automatic transmission. ATV riders shift a lever with their left foot for manual transmissions. Automatic transmissions switch gears without the driver shifting a lever.

ATV tires have thick treads to provide good traction on uneven surfaces. The tires are made of a soft rubber that gives them better grip. Tire sizes range from 18 to 27 inches (46 to 69 centimeters).

Traction Control

Some ATVs are two-wheel drive. Others are four-wheel drive. Power goes from the engine to the two rear wheels on two-wheel drive ATVs. Power goes to all four wheels on four-wheel drive ATVs.

The deep tread on ATV tires allows riders to get good traction.

Some ATVs are both two-wheel and four-wheel drive. Riders push a button to switch into four-wheel drive when they need good traction on rough or muddy ground.

The fastest ATVs can go 60 miles (100 kilometers) an hour or more.

Engines and Speed

Engine size is the main feature that affects an ATV's speed and power. ATV engines are measured in cubic centimeters (cc).

The smallest ATV engine is 50cc. These small engines are designed for riders as young as age six. A 50cc engine can power an ATV to speeds as fast as 15 miles (24 kilometers) an hour.

Midsize engines are between 200cc and 400cc. ATVs with engines this size can reach speeds of about 40 miles (64 kilometers) an hour. Farmers and ranchers often use these ATVs in their work.

Some ATV companies build 700cc engines. These big engines can produce speeds of 60 miles (100 kilometers) an hour or more. Search-and-rescue teams often use this type of ATV because they provide much needed power.

High-performance shock absorbers create
smoother rides on bumpy tracks.

Other Features

Racers modify ATVs by adding parts that were not included when the ATV was purchased. Riders call these parts high-performance parts because the parts add to the ATV's performance.

Some riders add high-performance shock absorbers and exhaust pipes. These extra parts help ATVs perform better in races. Shock absorbers lessen the impact that a rider feels when an ATV goes over bumps. Exhaust parts help engines get rid of waste when fuel is burned.

Riders may attach skidplates to the bottom of the ATV. The plates are made of strong metal. The plates protect the ATV from trail hazards such as rocks and fallen tree branches.

Learn about:

CHAPTER 4

ATVs in Competition

The American Motorcyclist Association (AMA) and the All Terrain Vehicle Association (ATVA) sponsor ATV races. Some races are national championships, such as the Grand National Motocross Championship and the Grand National Cross-Country.

ATV Tracks

ATV racers compete on many types of tracks. Different kinds of races are held on each type of track.

Small indoor tracks are called arenacross and supercross tracks. They have sharp twists, big jumps, and smaller bumps called whoop-de-dos.

Many races are held on outdoor tracks. Flat tracks are outdoor, hard-packed dirt tracks. These oval tracks only have left turns. Flat tracks that include left and right turns and small jumps are called tourist trophy (TT) tracks.

Motocross tracks are also outdoor tracks. These tracks are usually about 1 mile (1.6 kilometers) long. Many motocross tracks are set up on beaches.

Cross-country tracks are outdoors. They are often between 6 and 10 miles (9.7 and 16 kilometers) long. Cross-country courses include dirt mounds, mud holes, boulders, and streams. Signs with red arrows are posted on trees to show racers which way to go.

Some ATV riders practice for outdoor races by riding on a beach.

Series Events

A racing series is more than one race. The Clear Channel Pro Quads Indoor Series is made up of six races each year. Sponsors pay prize money to the top finishers at this series.

Series champions are decided based on how they race during the year. Racers earn points based on their finish in each race. The racer with the most points at the end of the season wins the series.

ATV riders choose ATVs that best fit the age group for each rider.

Safety

Safety is important for all ATV riders. Young riders should be extra careful. Less than 15 percent of ATV riders are younger than age 16. But this group accounts for nearly half of all injuries.

The ATV Safety Institute (ASI) has made riding safer. The group offers a free class for anyone who buys an ATV that fits the rider's age group. This class is called the ATV RiderCourse.

Safety equipment is a must for ATV riders. Riders should wear helmets and goggles. They also should wear knee and elbow pads, padded gloves, and high-top boots.

ATV riders are aware of their surroundings. Riders who use their ATVs in wilderness areas are careful not to damage trees and plants near ATV trails.

ATV riding is fun and rewarding. Riders who wear the right safety equipment and learn to ride properly enjoy good times on their ATVs.

Tim Farr

   Tim Farr is one of the best ATV racers in the world. He has won several national titles.

   Farr was born May 7, 1972, in North Kingsville, Ohio. He rode minibikes and motorcycles in gravel pits near his house. Tim and his older brother, Tom, repaired old motorcycles. Tim soon took part in organized motorcycle races.

   At age 17, Farr began racing ATVs. Two years later, he turned pro. He enjoyed working on engines, and he earned a mechanical engineering degree in college.

   In 1995, Farr won his first GNC Pro Champion title. He won it again in 1996 and 1998. He also won four Pro Quad Points Champion titles from 1999 to 2002.

Glossary

chassis (CHASS-ee)—the frame on which the body of an ATV is built

modify (MOD-uh-fye)—to change; racers modify an ATV body or engine to make it more powerful.

sponsor (SPAHN-sur)—to pay for and plan a race; ATVA sponsors races.

straightaway (STRAYT-uh-way)—a portion of a track without turns or obstacles

throttle (THROT-uhl)—the part of an ATV that controls the amount of fuel and air that flows into an engine

traction (TRAK-shuhn)—the grip of an ATV's tires on the ground

tread (TRED)—a series of deep grooves and bumps on a tire; tread helps tires grip rough surfaces.

Read More

Burch, Monte. *The Field & Stream All-Terrain Vehicle Handbook*. Guilford, Conn.: The Lyons Press, 2001.

McKenna, A.T. *Off-Road Racing*. Minneapolis: Abdo & Daughters, 1998.

Useful Addresses

All Terrain Vehicle Association
P.O. Box 800
Pickerington, OH 43147

ATV Connection Magazine
16135 Vintage Street NW
Andover, MN 55034

ATV Source Magazine
5586 Wanda Way
Hamilton, OH 45011-5094

Internet Sites

FactHound offers a safe, fun way to find Internet sites related to this book. All of the sites on FactHound have been researched by our staff.

Here's how:

1. Visit *www.facthound.com*

2. Type in this special code **0736824286** for age-appropriate sites. Or enter a search word related to this book for a more general search.

3. Click on the **Fetch It** button.

FactHound will fetch the best sites for you!

Index